Sid's Pet Rat

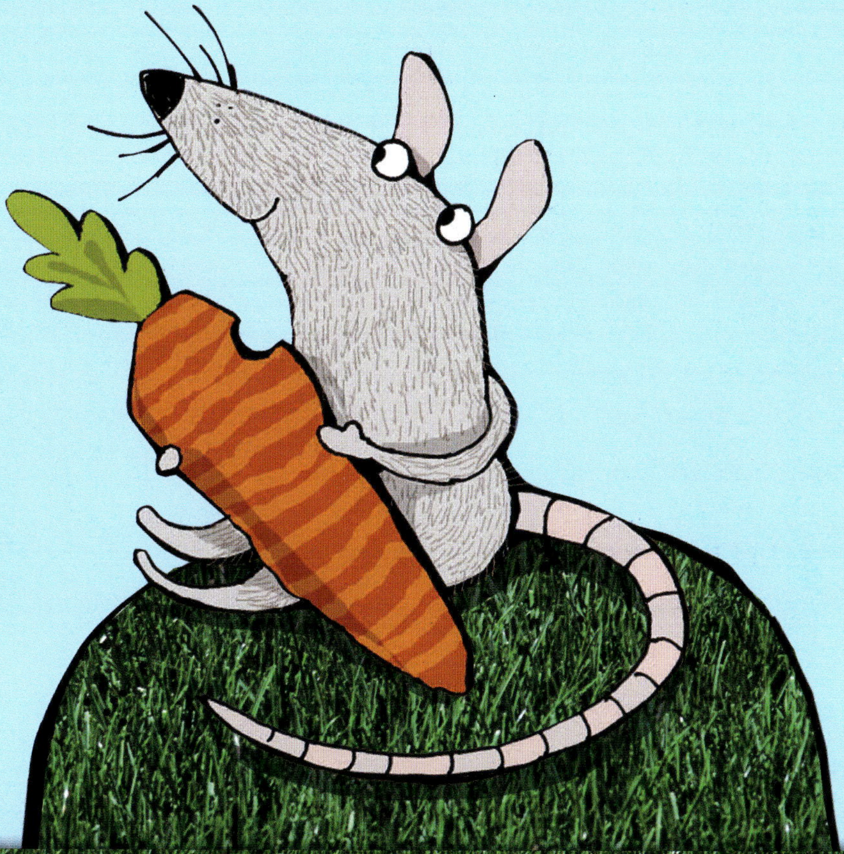

Written by Jeanne Willis
Illustrated by Jess Mikhail

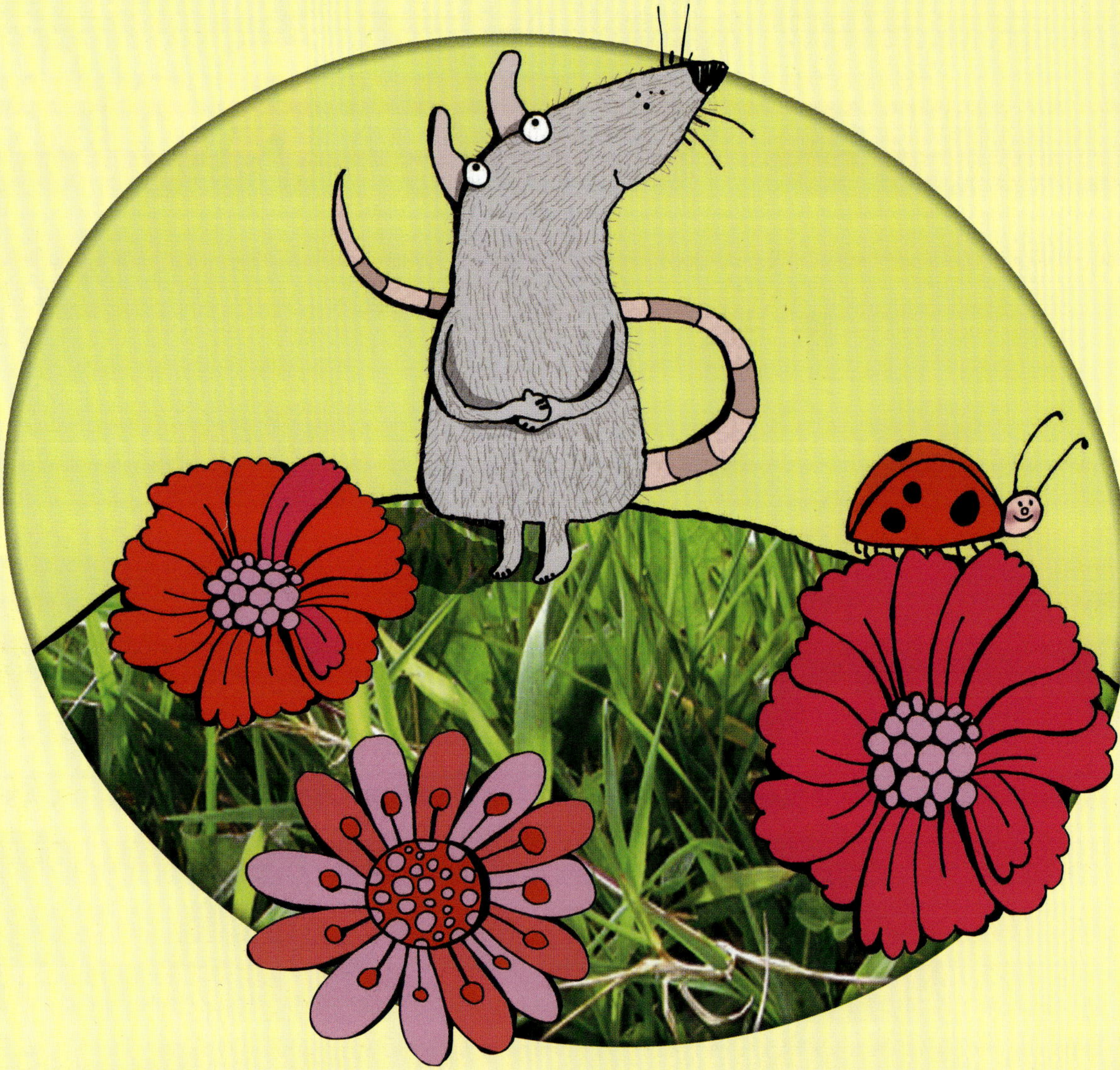

Sid's pet rat

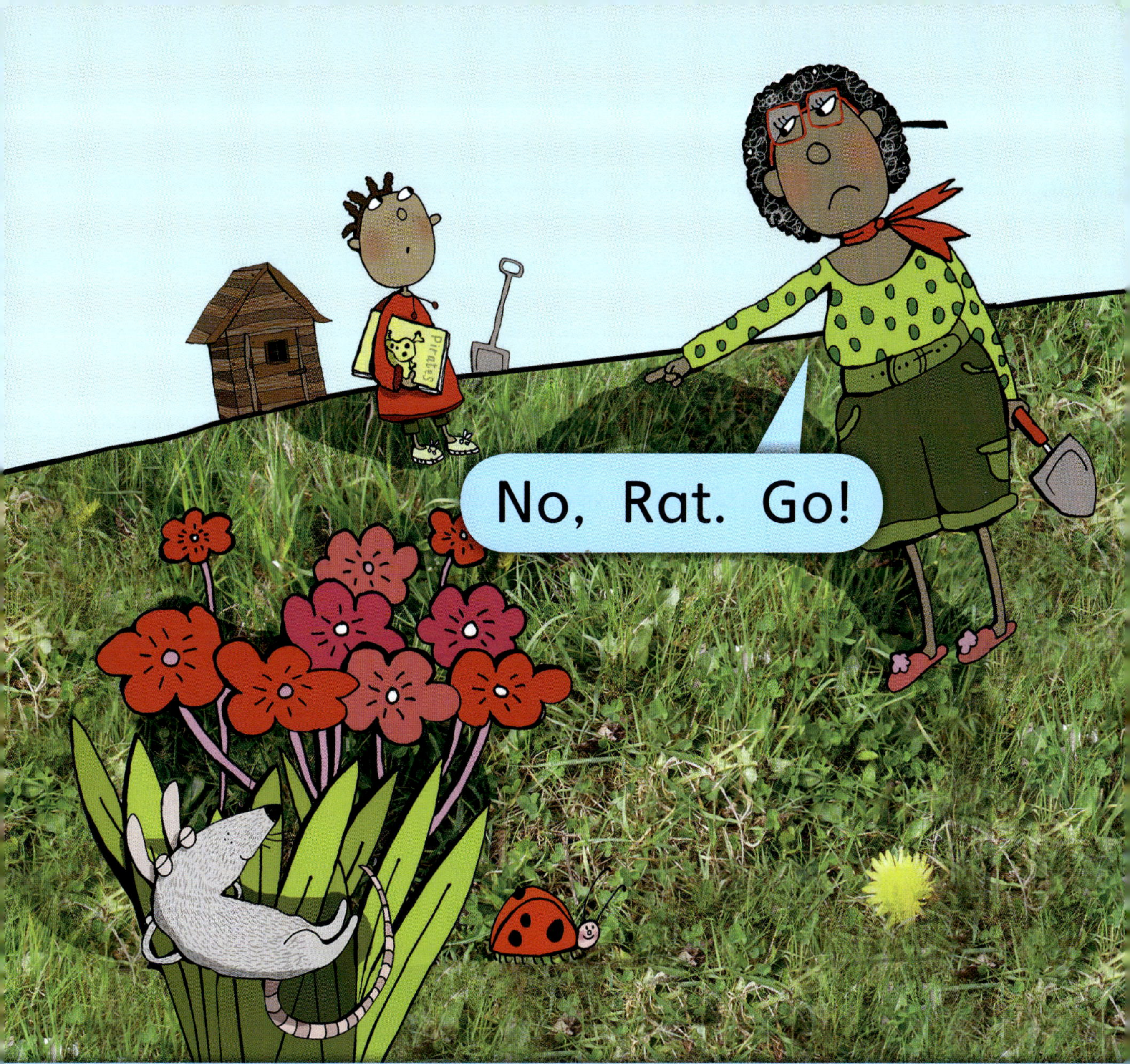

Rat sat in the sun.

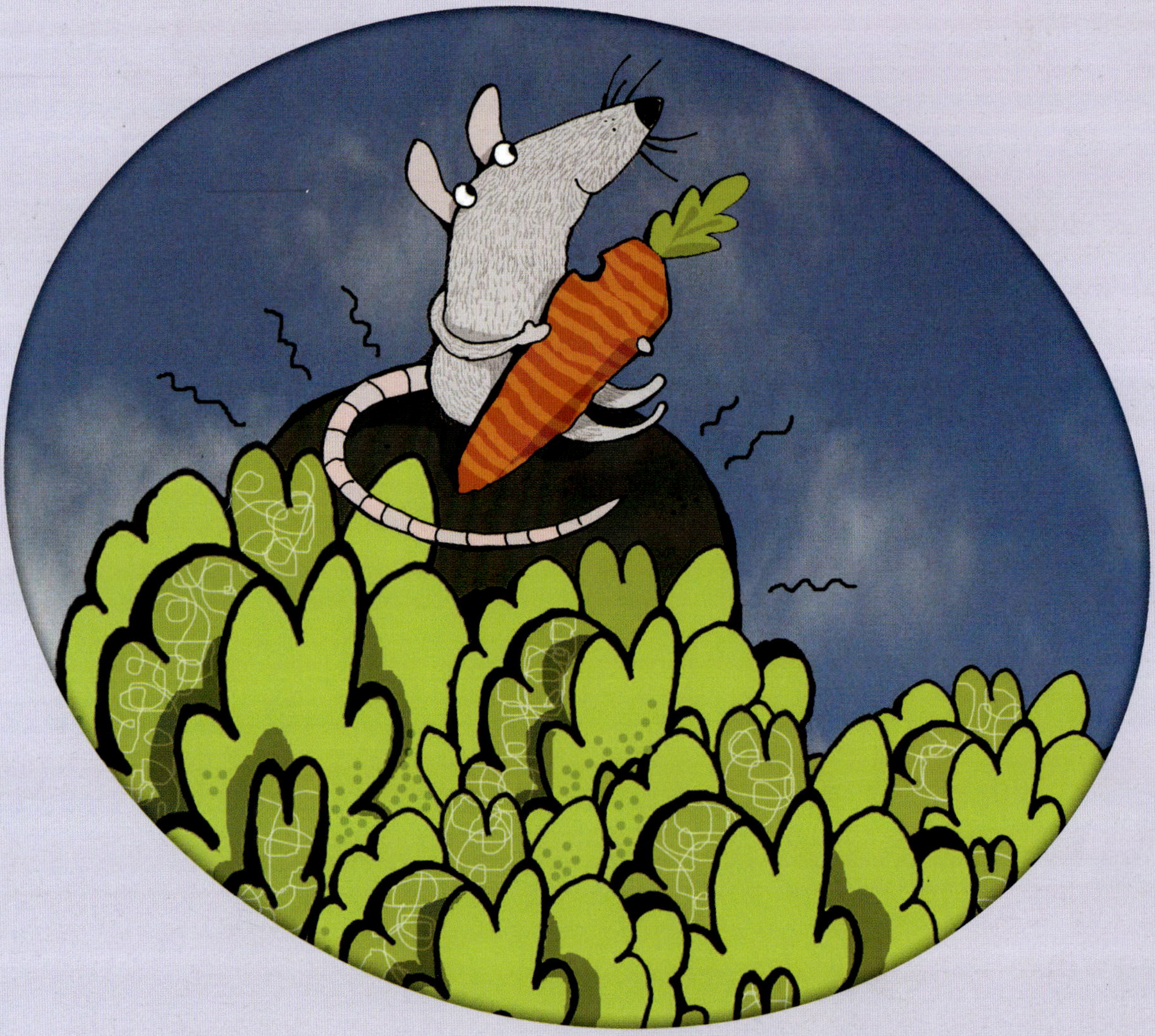

Rat sat in the muck.

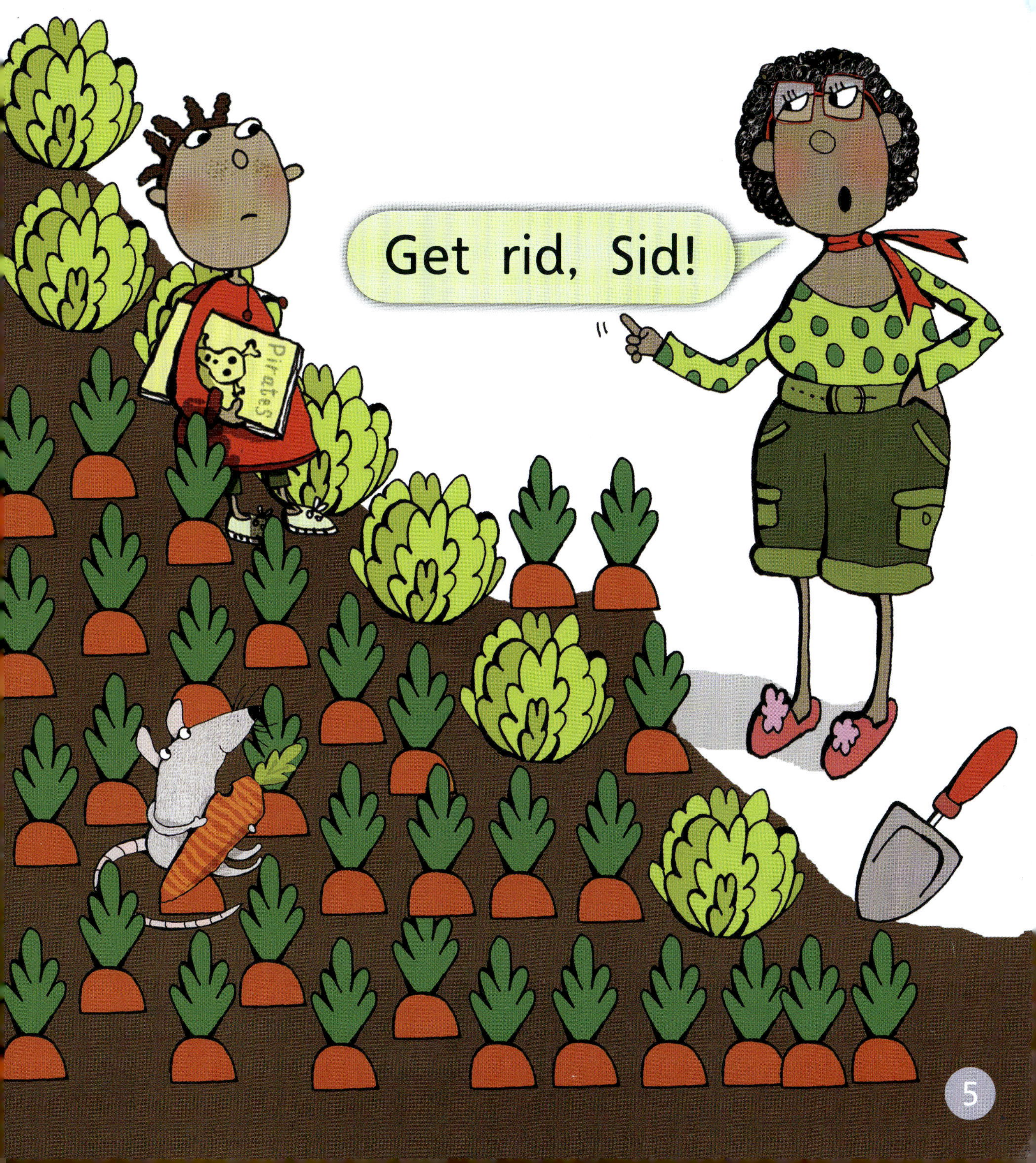
Get rid, Sid!
Pirates

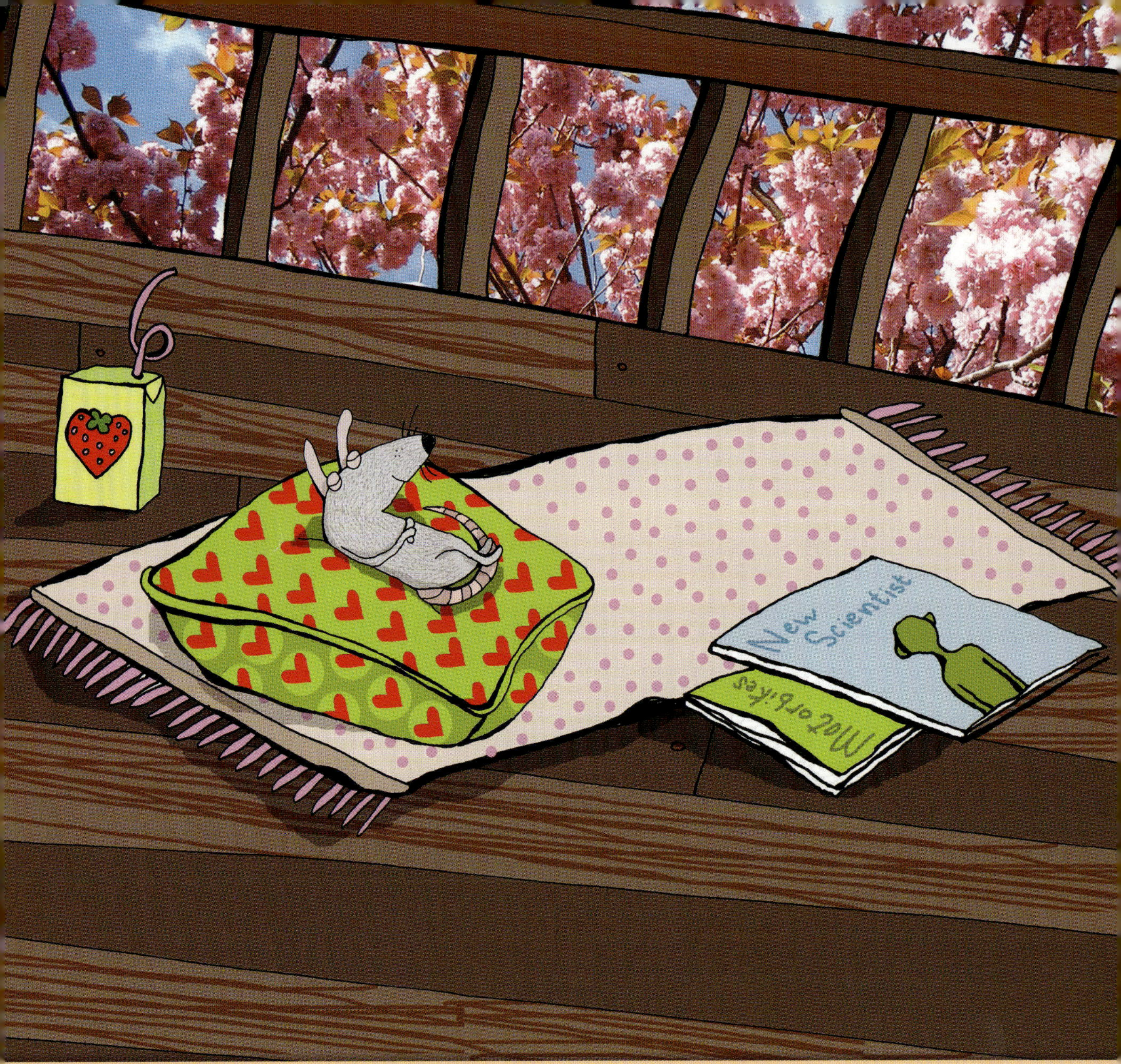

Rat sat on the deck.

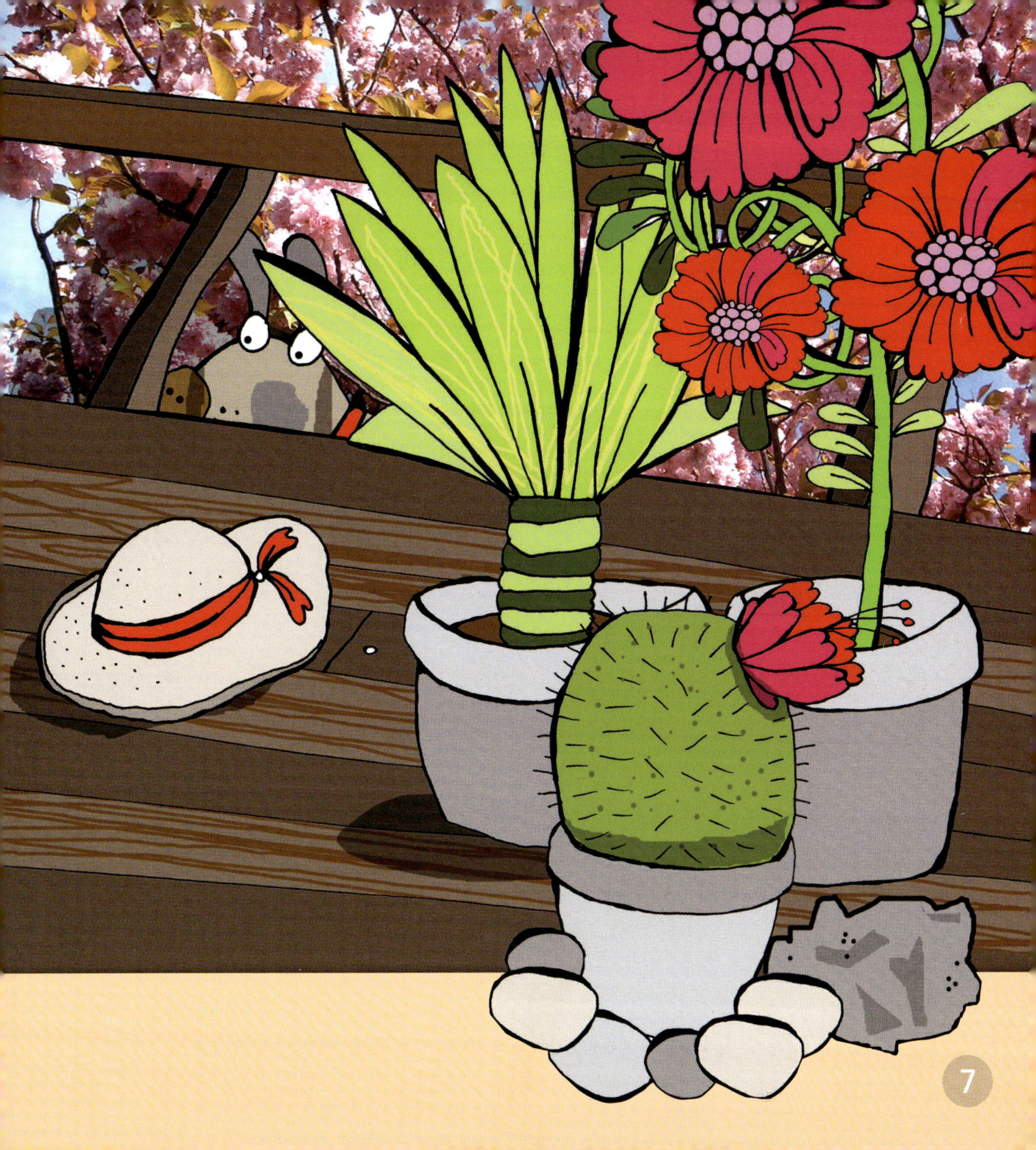

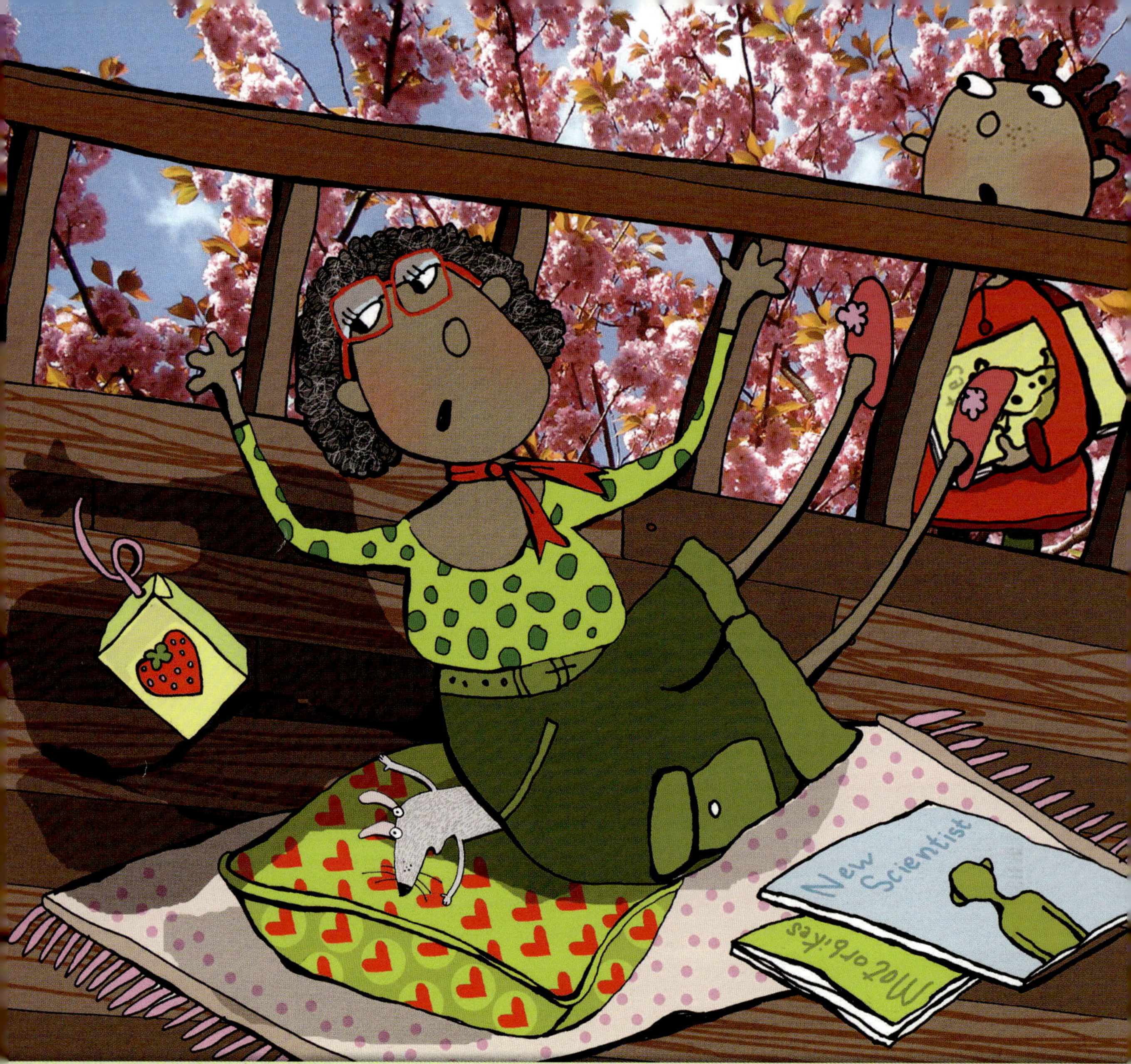

Nan sat on Rat!